Prologue

My name is Anthony Foley, and I'm a man who has lived many lives. From the steady beat of a snare drum in a high school drumline to the electrifying pulse of a club DJ set, I've always been driven by a love for music and performance. I sang in the choir, played guitar, and captured audiences as a drummer. I even found joy in the art of illusion as a magician, captivating audiences in clubs and festivals. Beyond music, I delved into photography and videography, capturing moments through lenses, and embraced the thrill of rugby and the laughter of comedy. Public speaking has also been a crucial part of my journey, allowing me to connect and inspire.

However, my journey hasn't been a seamless rhythm of success. Addiction entered my life, and one by one, my passions slipped away. My talents and drive became shadows of what they once were. The darkest chapter of my life involved the horrors of addiction, which spiraled into a void of despair, leading me to the brink of suicide. The night I overdosed is etched into my memory—a final, desperate attempt to escape the pain after another failed suicide attempt the day before. I woke up in a hospital, surrounded by white walls and a stark realization of how close I had come to losing everything.

Hitting rock bottom was a harsh mentor, but through recovery and faith in Jesus, I rediscovered my love for the arts and the powerful thrill of performing. Embracing spirituality brought profound change, guiding me toward a path of healing and purpose. I learned that resilience, like rhythm, isn't just about never missing a beat, but about finding your way back to the music after the silence of struggle.

After getting clean, I reclaimed my hobbies and started my own entertainment business. I turned my passions into a livelihood, living proof of the old saying: when you do what you love, you'll never work a day in your life. This book is a testament to the belief that our hobbies can not only save us but also support us.

Welcome to "Never Work a Day: Turn Your Hobbies into Cash." Let my story, the lessons I've learned, and the faith that guided me light your path to turning passion into profit.

A Journey Of Redemption

It was a story that began with a fracture, a split that tore through the fabric of my young life. At the tender age of four, my mother and father went their separate ways, leaving me in Ohio with my dad while my mom and two sisters ventured to Tennessee. Life was a delicate balance, constantly shifting between two worlds. Then, in August 2002, a sudden event shattered my reality. My father slipped into a coma, and I found myself uprooted once again, this time to be with my mother. Little did I know that this would mark the beginning of a journey filled with profound loss and eventual redemption.

The holiday season that year held a darkness I could not comprehend. Christmas arrived with a muted sorrow as my mother, shielding me from the harsh truth, chose to delay the news of my father's passing until the day after. The weight of his absence settled deep within me, casting a shadow over the joyous season.

Amidst the grief and confusion, I sought refuge in the arms of creativity and expression. Music became my sanctuary, a rhythmic heartbeat that soothed the ache in my soul. Joining the drumline in middle school, I found solace in the steady cadence of percussion. High school brought new avenues of exploration as I delved into the world of choir, my voice becoming a vessel for untold emotions. The allure of technology beckoned, leading me to immerse myself in computer classes and the captivating realm of videography. Each note, each image, each beat became a lifeline in the turbulent sea of my emotions.

Yet, as I navigated the waters of adolescence and young adulthood, a darker undertow threatened to pull me under. The vibrant lights of Atlanta's nightlife beckoned, promising escape and euphoria. It was amidst the pulsating energy of raves and festivals that I discovered a new passion—DJing. The music became a conduit for my inner turmoil, a soundtrack to the escalating battle with addiction that raged within me. Legal troubles loomed on the horizon, casting a long shadow over my budding dreams.

In the depths of despair, a flicker of light pierced through the darkness. A journey of faith and self-discovery unfolded, leading me to a place of reckoning and renewal. Homeless and adrift, I found myself seeking solace in the shelter of newfound spirituality. It was in those moments of vulnerability that I encountered a power greater than myself—a guiding force that would shape the course of my redemption.

But the road to recovery was far from smooth. Temptation whispered seductively, luring me back into old patterns of self-destruction. Lying to myself became second nature, a veil to shield me from confronting the truth. The cycle of addiction tightened its grip once more, threatening to drag me under its suffocating weight. In a moment of despair, I made a fateful decision—one that nearly cost me everything.

Waking up in a hospital room, the stark reality of my actions hit me with brutal clarity. The brink of oblivion had beckoned, but a higher power had other plans. Through the unwavering support of friends and the divine intervention of grace, I found a path back from the edge. Embracing a newfound sense of purpose, I made a vow to turn my life around and walk a different path—one illuminated by faith and resilience.

And so, from the ashes of my past emerged a new beginning. Determined to spread hope and joy, I founded Cope'N Entertainment, a beacon of light in a world shadowed by despair. My journey through the realms of music, performance, and marketing had led me to a place where I could not only heal myself but also extend a hand to others in need.

Venturing into the realm of freelance marketing, I embraced new horizons and opportunities with a renewed sense of purpose. DJing, performing in bands, motivational speaking—each endeavor became a testament to the transformative power of faith and perseverance. Creating social media content, organizing events, and practicing the art of magic, I discovered a multifaceted approach to spreading positivity and inspiration.

As I found my place at the Christian radio station that had once bridged the gap between my mother and me, I realized that my journey of redemption was far from over. It was a melody of resilience and rebirth, a symphony of hope and healing waiting to be shared with all who dared to listen. And so, with each beat of my heart and each word I spoke, I vowed to turn my past struggles into a beacon of light for those navigating the shadows of their own journeys.

Identifying Your Hobbies And Skills

As I emerged from the crucible of my past, a newfound sense of clarity and purpose guided my steps towards a brighter future. The journey of redemption had unearthed a treasure trove of passions and talents that lay dormant within me, waiting to be harnessed and transformed into sources of both joy and prosperity.

Assessing Your Interests and Talents

In the gentle embrace of self-discovery, I embarked on a journey of introspection, peeling back the layers of my being to reveal the core of my true passions. Music had always been a steadfast companion, a language of emotion that transcended words. The rhythmic pulse of the drum, the melodic strains of the guitar, the harmonious blend of voices in choir—each facet of my musical journey spoke volumes about my soul's deepest longings.

But beyond the realm of music, I found myself drawn to the art of performance—a stage where illusions came to life and laughter echoed through the night. The thrill of captivating an audience with magic, the adrenaline rush of rugby, the joy of spreading laughter through comedy—all these experiences wove a tapestry of diverse interests that colored the canvas of my existence.

Recognizing Potential Money-Making Hobbies

As I delved deeper into the labyrinth of my interests, a realization dawned upon me like a beacon in the night: these hobbies were not merely pastimes but potential pathways to financial abundance. The seeds of creativity and skill that I had nurtured over the years held the key to unlocking a world of opportunities for monetization and growth.

The rhythmic beats of the drumline could translate into lucrative gigs at events and gatherings, where my musical talents could shine and earn me a steady income. The mesmerizing art of magic, honed through years of practice and dedication, could captivate audiences not just for entertainment but also for profit. The world of photography and videography, where moments were frozen in time and emotions immortalized through lenses, offered a myriad of avenues for commercial success.

It became clear to me that the passions I had cultivated with such fervor and dedication had the potential to not only enrich my life spiritually and emotionally but also to serve as pillars of financial stability and independence. With this newfound awareness, I set forth on a quest to harness the power of my hobbies and skills, transforming them into sources of income and fulfillment.

In the realm of turning hobbies into cash, the first step lay in recognizing the intrinsic value of my interests and talents. By assessing the depths of my passions and acknowledging the potential they held for financial gain, I set the stage for a transformative journey of self-discovery and prosperity. With a heart full of hope and a mind open to possibilities, I embarked on a quest to unlock the hidden treasures of my soul and turn them into beacons of light in the world of entrepreneurship and creativity.

Researching Market Demands

As I navigated the landscape of turning my hobbies into profitable ventures, a crucial step beckoned on the horizon: understanding the intricate dance of market demand. The world of entrepreneurship and creativity was a dynamic realm, shaped by shifting trends and evolving opportunities. To carve a niche for myself and my passions, I delved into the realm of market research with a keen eye and a curious heart.

Understanding Market Trends and Opportunities

In the tapestry of commerce and creativity, market trends played a pivotal role in shaping the landscape of success and growth. With a discerning gaze, I scoured the horizons for signs and signals of emerging opportunities, seeking to align my passions with the currents of demand and preference.

The realm of music and performance, where my heart found solace and joy, was a vibrant tapestry of diverse genres and styles. By immersing myself in the pulse of the industry, I gleaned insights into the shifting tastes of audiences and the emerging trends that dictated the ebb and flow of creative expression. From the soaring heights of pop music to the soulful depths of jazz, each genre held its own allure and potential for commercial success.

In the realm of magic and illusion, where wonder and mystery danced hand in hand, I discovered a niche market brimming with untapped possibilities. The art of sleight of hand and the allure of grand illusions captivated audiences far and wide, offering a unique avenue for entertainment and entrepreneurship. By studying the patterns of demand and the preferences of consumers, I unearthed a treasure trove of opportunities waiting to be explored and exploited.

Identifying Niche Markets for Your Hobbies

As I ventured deeper into the realm of market research, a revelation dawned upon me: the power of niche markets to fuel the flames of success and prosperity. In the vast expanse of industries and sectors, niche markets offered a fertile ground for growth and innovation, providing a platform for unique voices and specialized offerings to thrive.

The world of music and performance, with its kaleidoscope of genres and styles, harbored niche markets waiting to be discovered and cultivated. From the enchanting realm of acoustic folk to the electrifying energy of EDM, each niche held its own audience and appeal, offering a niche market for specialized services and products. By honing in on these specific segments of the industry, I could tailor my offerings to cater to the unique needs and preferences of discerning consumers.

In the realm of magic and entertainment, the concept of niche markets took on a new dimension, offering a playground for innovation and experimentation. From the realm of close-up magic to the realm of stage illusions, each niche presented a canvas for creative expression and commercial success. By identifying these specialized markets and crafting offerings that resonated with their unique demands, I could carve a niche for myself in the competitive landscape of entertainment and entrepreneurship.

In the realm of turning hobbies into cash, the journey of researching market demand was a crucial step towards success and prosperity. By understanding the nuances of market trends and opportunities, and identifying niche markets for my passions, I set the stage for a transformative journey of growth and innovation. With a heart attuned to the rhythms of demand and a mind open to the possibilities of niche markets, I embarked on a quest to harness the power of market research and pave the way for a future brimming with potential and promise.

Building Your Brand

As I delved deeper into the realm of transforming my hobbies into profitable ventures, a pivotal chapter unfolded before me: the art of building a brand. In the tapestry of entrepreneurship and creativity, crafting a unique identity for my hobby-based business was a beacon of light, guiding me towards success and recognition. With a heart full of passion and a vision brimming with possibility, I set forth on a journey to establish a brand that would resonate with audiences far and wide.

Crafting a Unique Identity for Your Hobby-Based Business

In the crucible of creativity and commerce, the concept of branding held a transformative power, shaping perceptions and forging connections with consumers. As I embarked on the journey of building my brand, I sought to imbue it with the essence of my passions and talents, weaving a narrative that spoke to the soul of my audience.

The world of music and performance, where my heart found solace and joy, became the cornerstone of my brand identity. Drawing upon the rhythmic beats of the drumline, the soulful melodies of the guitar, and the harmonious blend of voices in choir, I crafted a brand that resonated with the emotions and aspirations of my audience. By infusing my brand with the essence of music and performance, I created a unique identity that set me apart in a sea of competitors.

In the realm of magic and entertainment, where wonder and mystery reigned supreme, I harnessed the power of storytelling and illusion to shape my brand identity. Drawing upon the art of sleight of hand and the allure of grand illusions, I crafted a brand that captivated the imagination and sparked curiosity. By infusing my brand with the magic of entertainment, I created a distinctive identity that left a lasting impression on audiences and clients alike.

Establishing a Strong Online and Offline Presence

With the foundation of my brand identity in place, I turned my focus towards establishing a strong online and offline presence that would amplify the reach of my hobby-based business. In the digital age of connectivity and engagement, a robust online presence was essential for building brand awareness and fostering customer relationships.

Through social media platforms and digital marketing strategies, I showcased the essence of my brand to a global audience, engaging with followers and fans in meaningful ways. From captivating photography and videography to engaging content and storytelling, I leveraged the power of online channels to amplify the voice of my brand and connect with audiences far and wide.

In the realm of offline presence, I turned towards cultivating meaningful relationships with local communities and industry partners, building a network of support and collaboration that bolstered the foundation of my brand. From hosting live events and performances to participating in industry conferences and networking opportunities, I embraced the power of face-to-face interactions to solidify the presence of my brand in the physical realm.

In the realm of turning hobbies into cash, the art of building a brand was a transformative journey of self-discovery and creativity. By crafting a unique identity for my hobby-based business and establishing a strong online and offline presence, I laid the groundwork for a future filled with promise and potential. With a heart attuned to the rhythms of branding and a vision set on the horizon of success, I embarked on a quest to build a brand that would resonate with audiences and stand the test of time.

Monetizing Your Hobbies

As I embarked on the journey of turning my hobbies into profitable ventures, the chapter of monetization beckoned me with promises of prosperity and fulfillment. The art of transforming passion into profit was a delicate dance of creativity and strategy, where exploring different revenue streams and implementing pricing strategies played a pivotal role in maximizing profitability. With a heart full of determination and a mind attuned to the nuances of commerce, I set forth on a quest to unlock the secrets of monetizing my hobbies.

Exploring Different Revenue Streams for Your Passions

In the realm of music and performance, where my soul found solace and joy, a myriad of revenue streams awaited exploration and exploitation. From live performances and gigs to music lessons and workshops, each avenue offered a unique opportunity to monetize my musical talents and passions. By diversifying my revenue streams and tapping into multiple channels of income, I could create a sustainable business model that transcended the constraints of traditional revenue models.

In the realm of magic and entertainment, where wonder and mystery reigned supreme, a treasure trove of revenue streams beckoned with promises of enchantment and prosperity. From corporate events and private parties to online tutorials and merchandise sales, each avenue presented a unique opportunity to monetize my magical talents and offerings. By harnessing the power of digital platforms and live performances, I could create a diverse portfolio of revenue streams that catered to a wide range of audiences and clients.

Pricing Strategies and Maximizing Profitability

With a diverse array of revenue streams at my disposal, the next step lay in implementing pricing strategies that maximized profitability and sustainability. In the realm of music and performance, where the value of artistry and creativity intersected with the principles of commerce, pricing strategies played a crucial role in balancing the scales of demand and profitability. By conducting market research and analyzing industry trends, I could set competitive pricing that reflected the value of my offerings while remaining accessible to a broad audience.

In the realm of magic and entertainment, where the allure of mystery and wonder captivated audiences far and wide, pricing strategies took on a new dimension of enchantment and intrigue. By pricing my services and products based on the perceived value and unique selling propositions, I could position myself as a premium provider in a competitive landscape. By offering tiered pricing options and bundled packages, I could cater to the diverse needs and preferences of clients while maximizing profitability and revenue potential.

In the realm of turning hobbies into cash, the chapter of monetization was a transformative journey of creativity and strategy. By exploring different revenue streams for my passions and implementing pricing strategies that maximized profitability, I set the stage for a future brimming with promise and prosperity. With a heart open to innovation and a mind sharp with strategy, I embarked on a quest to unlock the secrets of monetizing my hobbies and turning my dreams into reality.

Marketing And Promotion

As I navigated the realms of monetizing my hobbies and building a brand, the chapter of marketing and promotion emerged as a beacon of light, guiding me towards success and recognition. In the dynamic landscape of entrepreneurship and creativity, creating effective marketing campaigns for my hobby business and utilizing social media and networking to reach my target audience were essential pillars of growth and visibility. With a heart full of passion and a mind attuned to the nuances of communication, I set forth on a quest to unlock the secrets of marketing and promotion for my budding ventures.

Creating Effective Marketing Campaigns for Your Hobby Business

In the realm of music and performance, where the echoes of creativity and emotion reverberated through the air, creating effective marketing campaigns was a transformative journey of storytelling and engagement. By crafting compelling narratives and visual assets that resonated with the hearts and minds of my audience, I could create a buzz and excitement around my musical offerings. From captivating posters and flyers to engaging social media content and email campaigns, each touchpoint became a canvas for creativity and connection.

In the realm of magic and entertainment, where the allure of mystery and wonder captivated audiences far and wide, marketing campaigns took on a new dimension of enchantment and intrigue. By weaving a tapestry of curiosity and fascination through digital and traditional channels, I could create a sense of anticipation and excitement around my magical performances and services. From captivating teaser videos and behind-the-scenes glimpses to interactive social media campaigns and influencer partnerships, each marketing campaign became a stage for magic and entertainment.

Utilizing Social Media and Networking to Reach Your Target Audience

In the digital age of connectivity and engagement, social media and networking emerged as powerful tools for reaching and engaging with my target audience. By harnessing the power of platforms like Instagram, Facebook, and YouTube, I could amplify the reach of my brand and connect with audiences on a global scale. Through engaging content, live streams, and interactive posts, I could foster meaningful relationships with followers and fans, building a community of supporters and advocates for my hobby-based business.

In the realm of offline networking, where face-to-face interactions held a special allure and impact, I turned towards industry events, conferences, and local gatherings to expand my reach and visibility. By forging strategic partnerships and collaborations with like-minded businesses and influencers, I could tap into new audiences and markets, opening doors for growth and expansion. Through networking opportunities and community engagement, I could build a strong foundation of support and camaraderie that bolstered the presence of my brand in the physical realm.

In the realm of turning hobbies into cash, the chapter of marketing and promotion was a transformative journey of creativity and connection. By creating effective marketing campaigns for my hobby business and utilizing social media and networking to reach my target audience, I set the stage for a future brimming with promise and potential. With a heart open to innovation and a mind sharp with strategy, I embarked on a quest to unlock the secrets of marketing and promotion and pave the way for a future filled with success and recognition.

Managing Finances And Budgeting

As I embarked on the exhilarating journey of turning my hobbies into profitable ventures, the chapter of managing finances and budgeting unfolded before me like a roadmap to success and sustainability. In the ever-evolving landscape of entrepreneurship and creativity, financial planning for my hobby-based venture and implementing budgeting tips and strategies were essential components of building a solid foundation for growth and prosperity. With a heart full of determination and a mind attuned to the nuances of finance, I set forth on a quest to unlock the secrets of managing finances and budgeting for my burgeoning endeavors.

Financial Planning for Your Hobby-Based Venture

In the realm of music and performance, where the symphony of artistry and passion resonated through the air, financial planning became a crucial cornerstone of sustainability and growth. By setting clear financial goals and projections, I could chart a course towards profitability and success, ensuring that my musical endeavors thrived in a competitive landscape. From tracking income and expenses to forecasting revenue streams and investment opportunities, I delved into the realm of financial planning with a strategic eye and a disciplined approach.

In the realm of magic and entertainment, where the allure of mystery and wonder captivated audiences far and wide, financial planning took on a new dimension of enchantment and strategy. By analyzing costs and pricing structures, I could optimize profitability and maximize revenue potential, ensuring that my magical performances and services flourished in a dynamic market. With a keen eye on cash flow management and risk assessment, I navigated the complexities of financial planning with a steady hand and a forward-thinking mindset.

Budgeting Tips and Strategies for Sustainable Growth

With financial planning as my compass, I turned towards the realm of budgeting as a tool for sustainable growth and stability. In the realm of music and performance, where the rhythms of creativity and commerce intertwined, budgeting tips and strategies became essential for managing expenses and investments. By creating a detailed budget that aligned with my financial goals and projections, I could track spending and allocate resources effectively, ensuring that my musical ventures remained financially viable and sustainable.

In the realm of magic and entertainment, where the magic of performance and the logic of business converged, budgeting tips and strategies offered a roadmap for financial success and stability. By implementing cost-saving measures and expense tracking techniques, I could optimize profitability and minimize financial risks, ensuring that my magical endeavors thrived in a competitive landscape. With a focus on financial discipline and strategic planning, I navigated the realm of budgeting with a sense of purpose and determination, laying the groundwork for sustainable growth and prosperity.

In the realm of turning hobbies into cash, the chapter of managing finances and budgeting was a transformative journey of discipline and strategy. By implementing financial planning for my hobby-based venture and utilizing budgeting tips and strategies for sustainable growth, I set the stage for a future brimming with promise and prosperity. With a heart open to financial literacy and a mind sharp with strategic thinking, I embarked on a quest to unlock the secrets of managing finances and budgeting, paving the way for a future filled with success and stability.

Scaling Your Business

As I journeyed through the realms of monetizing my hobbies, building a brand, and navigating the intricacies of marketing and finance, the chapter of scaling my business emerged as a new horizon of growth and opportunity. In the ever-evolving landscape of entrepreneurship and creativity, expanding my hobby business and reaching new markets became essential steps towards unlocking the full potential of my passions. Through strategic planning and a mindset of innovation, I set forth on a quest to explore the avenues of scaling my business, embracing the challenges and opportunities that lay ahead.

Expanding Your Hobby Business and Reaching New Markets

In the realm of music and performance, where the melodies of creativity and passion intertwined, expanding my hobby business presented a myriad of possibilities for growth and impact. By exploring new markets and audiences, I could broaden the reach of my musical offerings and tap into untapped opportunities for collaboration and partnership.

From venturing into different genres and styles to expanding into new geographical locations, each expansion brought with it the promise of growth and discovery.

In the realm of magic and entertainment, where the allure of mystery and wonder captivated audiences far and wide, scaling my business opened doors to new realms of enchantment and excitement. By diversifying my services and offerings, I could cater to a wider range of clients and audiences, expanding the reach and impact of my magical performances. From exploring new performance venues and events to collaborating with industry influencers and partners, each step towards expansion brought with it the thrill of new possibilities and growth.

Outsourcing and Delegation for Efficiency

With the vision of scaling my business firmly in mind, I turned towards the realm of outsourcing and delegation as tools for efficiency and growth. In the realm of music and performance, where the demands of creativity and logistics intersected, outsourcing tasks like event planning, marketing, and administrative work could free up valuable time and resources, allowing me to focus on the core aspects of my musical endeavors. By delegating responsibilities to trusted partners and collaborators, I could streamline operations and maximize productivity, paving the way for sustainable growth and success.

In the realm of magic and entertainment, where the magic of performance and the logic of business intertwined, outsourcing and delegation offered a pathway towards efficiency and scalability. By outsourcing tasks like booking and scheduling, costume design, and technical support, I could optimize the performance of my magical endeavors and expand my reach to new markets and audiences. By leveraging the expertise and resources of external partners, I could unlock new opportunities for growth and innovation, propelling my hobby business towards new heights of success and recognition.

In the realm of turning hobbies into cash, the chapter of scaling my business was a transformative journey of growth and opportunity. By expanding my hobby business and reaching new markets, and embracing outsourcing and delegation for efficiency, I set the stage for a future brimming with promise and potential. With a heart open to innovation and a mind sharp with strategic thinking, I embarked on a quest to unlock the secrets of scaling my business, paving the way for a future filled with success and prosperity.

Customer Relations And Feedback

As I delved deeper into the realms of scaling my business and expanding my reach, the chapter of customer relations and feedback emerged as a cornerstone of success and sustainability. In the dynamic landscape of entrepreneurship and creativity, building strong relationships with my clients and utilizing feedback to improve my services and offerings became essential pillars of growth and excellence. With a heart full of empathy and a mind attuned to the needs of my audience, I set forth on a quest to unlock the secrets of customer relations and feedback, forging connections that would propel my hobby business towards new heights of success.

Building Strong Relationships with Your Clients

In the realm of music and performance, where the melodies of creativity and emotion resonated through the air, building strong relationships with my clients was a transformative journey of trust and connection. By prioritizing open communication and personalized experiences, I could forge lasting bonds with my audience, creating a loyal base of supporters and advocates for my musical endeavors. From offering exceptional customer service to tailoring performances to meet the unique needs and preferences of clients, each interaction became an opportunity to nurture relationships and foster loyalty.

In the realm of magic and entertainment, where the magic of performance and the wonder of imagination captivated audiences far and wide, building strong relationships with clients took on a new dimension of enchantment and connection. By creating memorable experiences and moments of delight, I could leave a lasting impression on my audience, garnering their trust and loyalty for future engagements. From personalized interactions and follow-ups to special offers and incentives, each touchpoint became a chance to deepen relationships and cultivate a community of supporters and fans.

Utilizing Feedback to Improve Your Services and Offerings

With a foundation of strong relationships in place, I turned towards the realm of feedback as a tool for continuous improvement and growth. In the realm of music and performance, where the nuances of artistry and expression intersected with the demands of audience expectations, feedback offered valuable insights into the impact and effectiveness of my musical offerings. By soliciting feedback from clients and audiences, I could gain a deeper understanding of their preferences and needs, allowing me to tailor my performances and services to better meet their expectations.

In the realm of magic and entertainment, where the magic of performance and the logic of business intertwined, feedback became a catalyst for innovation and excellence. By actively seeking feedback from clients and audiences, I could identify areas for improvement and opportunities for growth, ensuring that my magical performances and services remained relevant and impactful. By leveraging feedback to refine my offerings and enhance the customer experience, I could continuously evolve and adapt to the changing needs and preferences of my audience, solidifying my position as a trusted provider in the realm of entertainment.

In the realm of turning hobbies into cash, the chapter of customer relations and feedback was a transformative journey of connection and growth. By building strong relationships with my clients and utilizing feedback to improve my services and offerings, I set the stage for a future brimming with success and excellence. With a heart open to empathy and a mind sharp with insights, I embarked on a quest to unlock the secrets of customer relations and feedback, forging connections that would sustain my hobby business and propel it towards new heights of recognition and impact.

Diversifying And Innovating

As I navigated the intricate realms of customer relations and feedback, the chapter of diversifying and innovating emerged as a beacon of opportunity and evolution. In the ever-changing landscape of entrepreneurship and creativity, staying ahead of the curve in my hobby industry and exploring new opportunities for growth and innovation became essential strategies for maintaining relevance and sustainability. With a heart full of curiosity and a mind attuned to the rhythms of change, I set forth on a quest to unlock the secrets of diversifying and innovating, embracing the challenges and possibilities that lay ahead.

Staying Ahead of the Curve in Your Hobby Industry

In the realm of music and performance, where the melodies of creativity and expression resonated through the air, staying ahead of the curve in my hobby industry was a journey of continuous learning and adaptation. By staying abreast of industry trends and emerging technologies, I could anticipate shifts in audience preferences and market dynamics, positioning my musical endeavors for success and relevance. From attending industry conferences and workshops to networking with industry leaders and influencers, each opportunity became a chance to gain insights and perspectives that would guide my strategic decisions and innovations.

In the realm of magic and entertainment, where the allure of mystery and wonder captivated audiences far and wide, staying ahead of the curve meant embracing a spirit of innovation and creativity. By exploring new magical techniques and performance styles, I could push the boundaries of my craft and captivate audiences with fresh and exciting experiences. From collaborating with fellow magicians and performers to experimenting with new technologies and storytelling formats, each endeavor became an opportunity to break new ground and set new standards in the realm of entertainment.

Exploring New Opportunities for Growth and Innovation

With a spirit of exploration and innovation guiding my path, I turned towards the realm of diversification as a strategy for growth and evolution. In the realm of music and performance, where the possibilities of expression and collaboration were endless, diversifying my offerings and services opened new avenues for revenue and impact. By exploring new genres and performance formats, I could cater to a wider range of audiences and expand my reach to untapped markets. From offering music lessons and workshops to collaborating with other artists and musicians, each new opportunity became a chance to diversify my portfolio and unlock new streams of income and engagement.

In the realm of magic and entertainment, where the magic of performance and the logic of business intersected, diversification became a key strategy for staying relevant and competitive. By exploring new performance styles and formats, I could captivate audiences with fresh and innovative experiences that set me apart from the competition. From offering themed magic shows and interactive experiences to venturing into new markets and industries, each new opportunity became a chance to innovate and diversify my offerings, propelling my hobby business towards new heights of success and recognition.

In the realm of turning hobbies into cash, the chapter of diversifying and innovating was a transformative journey of growth and evolution. By staying ahead of the curve in my hobby industry and exploring new opportunities for growth and innovation, I set the stage for a future brimming with possibility and potential. With a heart open to exploration and a mind sharp with creativity, I embarked on a quest to unlock the secrets of diversifying and innovating, embracing the challenges and opportunities that would shape the future of my hobby business and propel it towards new heights of success and impact.

Conclusion

As I reflect on the transformative journey of turning my hobbies into profitable ventures, the chapters of entrepreneurship, creativity, and innovation unfold like a tapestry of growth and evolution. From the inception of building a brand and monetizing my passions to the complexities of marketing, finance, and customer relations, each chapter offered valuable lessons and insights that shaped my path towards success and sustainability. Through perseverance, resilience, and a spirit of curiosity, I navigated the challenges and opportunities that came my way, embracing the dynamics of change and adaptation as I forged a path towards a future filled with promise and potential.

The journey of entrepreneurship taught me the importance of resilience and adaptability in the face of uncertainty and challenges. By embracing a mindset of innovation and creativity, I discovered new opportunities for growth and evolution, propelling my hobby-based ventures towards new heights of success and recognition. Through strategic planning, financial discipline, and customer-centric approaches, I built a solid foundation for sustainable growth and profitability, setting the stage for a future filled with possibilities and opportunities.

As I ventured into the realms of marketing and customer relations, I learned the value of building strong relationships with clients and leveraging feedback to improve my services and offerings. By prioritizing empathy, communication, and continuous improvement, I cultivated a loyal base of supporters and advocates who propelled my hobby businesses towards new levels of success and impact. Through a commitment to excellence and a dedication to authenticity, I forged connections that sustained my ventures and paved the way for future growth and expansion.

The chapters of scaling my business, diversifying, and innovating offered a roadmap towards staying ahead of the curve in my hobby industry and exploring new opportunities for growth and evolution. By embracing change and pushing the boundaries of creativity, I unlocked new streams of revenue and engagement, propelling my endeavors towards new heights of success and recognition. Through a spirit of exploration, innovation, and strategic planning, I navigated the complexities of entrepreneurship with a sense of purpose and determination, shaping a future brimming with promise and potential.

As I close this chapter of my journey towards turning hobbies into profitable ventures, I carry with me the lessons and experiences that have shaped my path towards success and sustainability. With a heart full of gratitude and a mind attuned to the rhythms of growth and evolution, I look towards the horizon with a sense of anticipation and excitement, ready to embrace the challenges and opportunities that lie ahead. Through a commitment to excellence, innovation, and authenticity, I embark on a new chapter of creativity, entrepreneurship, and fulfillment, confident in the knowledge that the best is yet to come.

I invite you, dear reader, to continue to part two of this book where I delve deeper into hobbies you might have and provide an in-depth model you can follow to turn your own passions into profitable ventures. Join me on a journey where you can "never have to work a day" as you monetize your hobbies and find fulfillment in pursuing your passions. The adventure awaits, and the possibilities are endless. Let's embark on this journey together and unlock the potential within you to turn your hobbies into cash.

Part 2

How to turn YOUR Hobbies into cash

Introduction

In today's fast-paced world, the idea of turning your hobbies into a source of income has become increasingly popular. The concept of using hobbies to generate income is not just a pipe dream but a viable opportunity for individuals to pursue their passions while also making money. In this chapter, we will delve into the definition of this concept, explore the benefits of monetizing your hobbies, and set realistic expectations for the process ahead.

Defining the Concept

At its core, using hobbies to generate income involves leveraging your interests, skills, and talents to create products or offer services that others are willing to pay for. Instead of viewing hobbies as mere pastimes or leisure activities, individuals can transform their hobbies into profitable ventures that not only bring personal fulfillment but also financial rewards. Whether you have a knack for crafting, a passion for photography, or a talent for cooking, there are countless opportunities to monetize your hobbies and turn your creative pursuits into a sustainable income stream.

The beauty of monetizing your hobbies lies in the ability to blend work and pleasure seamlessly. By combining your passion with entrepreneurship, you can create a fulfilling career that aligns with your interests and values. Rather than feeling trapped in a job that lacks meaning or excitement, pursuing a hobby-based income allows you to showcase your unique talents and share your creativity with the world.

Exploring the Benefits

There are numerous benefits to turning your hobbies into a source of income, both personally and professionally. One of the most significant advantages is the opportunity to do what you love while earning money. Instead of dreading Mondays and counting down the hours until the weekend, you can wake up each day excited to work on projects that bring you joy and fulfillment.

Monetizing your hobbies also offers a sense of autonomy and control over your career. Rather than being subject to the demands of a boss or company, you are the master of your own destiny. You can set your own schedule, choose the projects you want to work on, and take your business in any direction you desire. This freedom and flexibility can lead to a greater sense of satisfaction and work-life balance.

Additionally, generating income from your hobbies can provide a valuable source of supplemental or even primary income. Whether you are looking to make some extra cash on the side or pursue a full-time career based on your passions, the potential for financial success is vast. By tapping into niche markets or catering to specific customer needs, you can create a lucrative business that aligns with your interests and skills.

Setting Realistic Expectations

While the idea of monetizing your hobbies may sound appealing, it is essential to set realistic expectations for the journey ahead. Turning your hobbies into a source of income is not a get-rich-quick scheme or an easy path to success. It requires dedication, hard work, and a willingness to learn and adapt along the way.

It is important to recognize that building a business based on your hobbies takes time and effort. Overnight success is rare, and most successful entrepreneurs experience setbacks and challenges before achieving their goals. Setting realistic expectations means understanding that there will be ups and downs, and that progress may be slow at times. However, by staying focused, persistent, and resilient, you can overcome obstacles and make your hobby-based income a reality.

In conclusion, the concept of using hobbies to generate income offers a world of possibilities for individuals seeking to combine passion with profit. By defining this concept, exploring its benefits, and setting realistic expectations, you can embark on a journey of creativity, entrepreneurship, and financial reward. As we delve deeper into the process of monetizing your hobbies in the chapters ahead, remember that success is within reach for those who are willing to put in the work and follow their dreams.

Identifying Your Profitable Hobbies

In Chapter 1, we discussed the concept of using hobbies to generate income and the benefits of turning your passions into a source of revenue. Now, we will delve into the process of identifying your profitable hobbies. This chapter will explore various types of hobbies that can be monetized, offer guidance on how to pinpoint your own money-making interests, and provide exercises to assess the income potential of your hobbies.

List of Different Types of Hobbies that Can Be Monetized

1. Arts and Crafts: Hobbies such as painting, pottery, knitting, and jewelry making can be monetized through selling handmade products online, at craft fairs, or through personalized commissions.

2. Photography: If you have a passion for photography, you can sell your prints, offer photography services for events, or create digital products like presets or tutorials.

3. Writing: Whether you enjoy writing fiction, non-fiction, poetry, or blog posts, there are opportunities to monetize your writing through self-publishing books, freelance writing, or content creation for businesses.

4. Cooking and Baking: If you love to cook or bake, you can start a food blog, offer cooking classes, sell homemade goods at farmers' markets, or cater events.

5. Fitness and Wellness: Hobbies like yoga, personal training, or nutrition coaching can be monetized through offering online classes, creating workout programs, or providing one-on-one coaching services.

6. Gardening: If you have a green thumb, you can sell plants, seeds, or gardening tools, offer landscaping services, or create an online gardening course.

7. Music: Whether you play an instrument, sing, or produce music, you can monetize your musical talents through live performances, teaching lessons, selling music online, or composing for films and commercials.

8. Technology: Hobbies related to technology, such as coding, graphic design, or video editing, can be monetized through freelance work, creating digital products, or offering online courses.

9. Travel: If you enjoy traveling, you can monetize your experiences through travel blogging, vlogging, affiliate marketing with travel brands, or organizing group tours.

10. DIY and Home Improvement: Hobbies like woodworking, home renovation, or upcycling furniture can be monetized by selling handmade goods, offering workshops, or providing home improvement services.

Helping Readers Identify Their Profitable Hobbies

Identifying your profitable hobbies is the first step towards building a successful business based on your passions. Here are some tips to help you pinpoint which hobbies have the potential to generate income:

1. Reflect on Your Interests: Take some time to reflect on the activities that bring you joy and fulfillment. What hobbies do you find yourself immersed in for hours on end? What skills do you possess that others may find valuable?

2. Consider Market Demand: Research the market demand for products or services related to your hobbies. Are there existing businesses or entrepreneurs successfully monetizing similar hobbies? Is there a niche or gap in the market that you can fill with your unique offerings?

3. Evaluate Your Skills: Assess your skills and expertise in your chosen hobbies. Do you have the necessary knowledge and experience to create high-quality products or offer valuable services? Are there areas where you can improve or expand your skill set?

4. Explore Your Network: Reach out to friends, family, or colleagues who know you well and ask for their input on your hobbies. They may offer valuable insights or suggestions that can help you identify which hobbies have the most potential for monetization.

5. Test the Waters: Consider testing the market for your hobbies before fully committing to monetizing them. This could involve creating a small batch of products to sell, offering trial services to a few clients, or launching a pilot program to gauge interest and feedback.

Exercises to Explore the Income Potential of Your Hobbies

To further explore the income potential of your hobbies, consider the following exercises:

1. Create a Hobby Inventory: Make a list of all your hobbies and interests, no matter how big or small. Rank them based on your level of passion and proficiency in each activity.

2. Conduct Market Research: Research the market demand and competition for products or services related to your top hobbies. Identify potential target audiences, pricing strategies, and distribution channels.

3. Develop a Business Idea: Based on your hobby inventory and market research, brainstorm potential business ideas that align with your interests and skills. Consider different revenue streams, such as selling products, offering services, or creating digital content.

4. Set Income Goals: Define your income goals and financial targets for each hobby-based business idea. Determine how much revenue you need to generate to make your venture sustainable and profitable.

5. Seek Feedback: Share your business ideas with trusted friends, mentors, or potential customers to gather feedback and insights. Use their input to refine your concepts and identify areas for improvement.

6. Calculate Costs and Pricing: Determine the costs associated with producing or offering your hobby-based products or services. Factor in materials, time, labor, overhead expenses, and any other costs

involved. Use this information to set competitive yet profitable pricing for your offerings.

7. Create a Prototype or Sample: Develop a prototype, sample, or mock-up of your product or service to showcase to potential customers. This tangible representation can help you gather feedback, refine your offerings, and attract early adopters.

8. Identify Distribution Channels: Explore different distribution channels for selling your products or services, such as online marketplaces, social media platforms, physical stores, or direct sales. Choose channels that align with your target audience and business goals.

9. Build a Brand Identity: Define your brand identity, including your values, mission, vision, and unique selling proposition (USP). Create a distinct and memorable brand that resonates with your target market and sets you apart from competitors.

10. Develop a Marketing Strategy: Outline a comprehensive marketing strategy to promote your hobby-based business and attract customers. Consider using a mix of online and offline tactics, such as social media marketing, email campaigns, influencer partnerships, and community events.

11. Set Up Financial Tracking: Implement systems to track your income, expenses, and profits related to your hobby-based business. Use accounting software, spreadsheets, or financial apps to monitor your financial performance and make informed decisions.

12. Seek Professional Advice: Consider consulting with mentors, coaches, or experts in your industry to gain valuable insights and

guidance on monetizing your hobbies. Learn from their experiences, mistakes, and successes to accelerate your own path to profitability.

By completing these exercises and taking a strategic approach to exploring the income potential of your hobbies, you can gain clarity, confidence, and direction in turning your passions into a profitable venture. Remember that the key to success lies in identifying hobbies that not only bring you joy but also resonate with your target market and have the potential to generate sustainable income over the long term.

In the upcoming chapters, we will further explore how to refine your business ideas, develop a solid plan for monetizing your hobbies, and execute strategies to grow your hobby-based income stream. Stay tuned for practical tips, real-life examples, and actionable advice to help you navigate the exciting journey of transforming your hobbies into a source of revenue.

Research And Planning

In Chapter 2, we explored the process of identifying profitable hobbies and assessing their income potential. Now, we will delve into the crucial steps of research and planning to lay the foundation for turning your hobbies into a sustainable source of income. This chapter will teach readers how to conduct market research on their chosen hobby, guide them in creating a comprehensive business plan, and discuss the importance of setting goals and milestones to track progress and measure success.

Conducting Market Research on Your Chosen Hobby

Market research is a critical component of building a successful business based on your hobbies. By understanding your target market, competitors, trends, and customer needs, you can make informed decisions and tailor your offerings to meet demand. Here are some steps to help you conduct market research on your chosen hobby:

1. Define Your Target Audience: Identify the demographic, psychographic, and behavioral characteristics of your ideal customers. Understand their preferences, pain points, buying habits, and motivations to create products or services that resonate with their needs and desires.

2. Analyze Competitor Landscape: Research existing businesses, brands, and individuals in your niche or industry. Identify your direct and indirect competitors, assess their strengths and weaknesses, and differentiate your offerings to stand out in the market.

3. Explore Industry Trends: Stay up-to-date on the latest industry trends, market dynamics, and consumer preferences related to your hobby. Monitor changes in technology, consumer behavior, regulations, and competitive landscape to adapt your business strategy accordingly.

4. Gather Customer Feedback: Conduct surveys, interviews, focus groups, or beta testing with potential customers to gather feedback on your hobby-based products or services. Use this valuable input to refine your offerings, address customer pain points, and enhance the overall customer experience.

5. Study Pricing Strategies: Research pricing strategies and benchmarks in your industry to determine the optimal pricing for your products or services. Consider factors such as cost of goods sold, competitor pricing, perceived value, and customer willingness to pay when setting your prices.

6. Identify Distribution Channels: Explore different distribution channels to reach your target audience and sell your products or services. Consider online platforms, physical stores, marketplaces, social media, events, or partnerships that align with your business goals and customer preferences.

7. Monitor Marketing Tactics: Analyze successful marketing tactics, campaigns, and promotions used by competitors or industry leaders

in your niche. Identify effective strategies for brand awareness, customer acquisition, engagement, and retention to inform your own marketing efforts.

By conducting thorough market research on your chosen hobby, you can gain valuable insights, identify opportunities, mitigate risks, and make data-driven decisions to maximize the success of your hobby-based income stream.

Creating a Business Plan for Your Hobby-Based Income Stream

A well-crafted business plan is essential for guiding the development, growth, and sustainability of your hobby-based income stream. A business plan serves as a roadmap that outlines your business goals, strategies, financial projections, and operational details. Here is a step-by-step guide to help you create a comprehensive business plan:

1. Executive Summary: Provide a concise overview of your business concept, mission, vision, goals, target market, unique selling proposition, and key highlights of your business plan.

2. Business Description: Describe your hobby-based business in detail, including the products or services you offer, your value proposition, competitive advantage, and the problem you aim to solve for your customers.

3. Market Analysis: Present the results of your market research, including industry trends, target audience demographics, competitor analysis, customer needs, market size, and growth opportunities in your niche.

4. Marketing and Sales Strategy: Outline your marketing and sales tactics for promoting your hobby-based products or services, acquiring customers, building brand awareness, and driving revenue growth. Include strategies for pricing, distribution, promotion, and customer retention.

5. Operational Plan: Detail the operational aspects of your business, such as production processes, supply chain management, inventory control, quality assurance, customer service, and fulfillment logistics. Explain how you will deliver value to customers efficiently and effectively.

6. Financial Projections: Create financial projections for your hobby-based income stream, including revenue forecasts, expense estimates, profit margins, cash flow projections, break-even analysis, and return on investment. Consider different scenarios, risks, and contingencies to ensure financial viability.

7. Implementation Plan: Develop a timeline, action plan, and milestones for launching and scaling your hobby-based business. Define specific tasks, responsibilities, deadlines, and performance metrics to guide your progress and measure success.

8. Legal and Regulatory Compliance: Ensure that your hobby-based business complies with relevant laws, regulations, permits, licenses, taxes, and intellectual property rights. Consult legal and financial advisors to address any legal or compliance issues proactively.

9. Risk Management: Identify potential risks, challenges, and uncertainties that may impact your hobby-based income stream. Develop risk mitigation strategies, contingency plans, and crisis management protocols to minimize negative outcomes and protect

Building Your Brand

In Chapter 3, we discussed the significance of conducting thorough research and creating a detailed business plan to turn your hobbies into a sustainable source of income. Now, we will explore the critical aspect of building your brand. Branding is a fundamental element in establishing a successful business based on your hobbies. In this chapter, we will explain the importance of branding, help readers define their unique selling proposition (USP), and provide tips on creating a strong brand identity that resonates with customers and sets your business apart from competitors.

The Importance of Branding in Turning Hobbies into Income

Branding plays a pivotal role in transforming hobbies into income-generating ventures. Your brand is more than just a logo or a name; it is the overall experience and perception that customers have of your business. A strong brand can differentiate your offerings, build trust and credibility, attract loyal customers, and ultimately drive revenue growth. Here are some key reasons why branding is crucial in monetizing your hobbies:

1. Differentiation: In a crowded marketplace, a strong brand helps you stand out from competitors and capture the attention of your target audience. By defining what makes your business unique and communicating it effectively, you can differentiate yourself and create a memorable impression in the minds of customers.

2. Trust and Credibility: A well-established brand instills trust and credibility in customers, making them more likely to engage with your products or services. Consistent branding signals professionalism, reliability, and quality, fostering positive perceptions and building long-term relationships with customers.

3. Emotional Connection: Effective branding evokes emotions and connects with customers on a deeper level. By conveying your values, personality, and story through your brand, you can create a meaningful bond with customers, leading to increased loyalty, advocacy, and repeat business.

4. Recognition and Recall: A strong brand identity makes your business easily recognizable and memorable to customers. Consistent branding across all touchpoints, from your logo and colors to your messaging and packaging, reinforces brand recall and strengthens brand awareness in the minds of consumers.

5. Pricing Power: A well-positioned brand can command premium pricing and higher perceived value in the eyes of customers. By cultivating a strong brand image and reputation, you can justify higher prices, attract discerning customers, and increase profitability for your hobby-based business.

6. Growth and Expansion: A solid brand foundation sets the stage for long-term growth and expansion opportunities. A strong brand identity facilitates entry into new markets, introduction of new products or services, partnerships with other brands, and scaling your business to new heights.

By understanding the importance of branding and leveraging it effectively in your hobby-based income stream, you can create a compelling brand that resonates with customers, drives sales, and establishes a strong market presence.

Defining Your Unique Selling Proposition (USP)

Your unique selling proposition (USP) is the specific value proposition that sets your business apart from competitors and provides a compelling reason for customers to choose your products or services. Your USP encapsulates what makes your business unique, relevant, and valuable to customers. Here are some steps to help you define your USP for your hobby-based income stream:

1. Identify Your Strengths: Reflect on your strengths, skills, expertise, and resources that differentiate your business from others in your niche. What unique qualities, talents, or experiences do you bring to the table that can add value to customers?

2. Understand Customer Needs: Put yourself in the shoes of your target customers and identify their unmet needs, pain points, desires, and preferences. How can your hobby-based products or services address these needs and provide solutions that resonate with customers?

3. Analyze Competitor Offerings: Research your competitors and assess their strengths, weaknesses, and offerings in the market. Identify opportunities to differentiate your business by offering something distinct, innovative, or superior that competitors do not provide.

4. Define Your Value Proposition: Articulate your value proposition by clearly stating the benefits, advantages, and outcomes that customers can expect from choosing your business over others.

What tangible and intangible value do you offer that makes your business compelling and irresistible to customers?

5. Communicate Your USP: Once you have defined your USP, incorporate it into your branding, messaging, marketing materials, and customer interactions. Consistently communicate your USP across all touchpoints to reinforce your unique value proposition and resonate with customers.

6. Test and Refine: Continuously test and refine your USP based on customer feedback, market trends, and competitive dynamics. Stay agile and adaptable in adjusting your USP to align with changing customer needs and evolving market conditions.

By defining a clear and compelling USP for your hobby-based income stream, you can effectively differentiate your business, attract customers, and create a strong competitive advantage in the marketplace.

Tips on Creating a Strong Brand Identity

A strong brand identity is the visual and verbal representation of your brand that communicates your values, personality, and story to customers. It encompasses elements such as your logo, colors, typography, imagery, messaging, and overall aesthetic that collectively convey the essence of your brand. Here are some tips on creating a strong brand identity for your hobby-based business:

1. Define Your Brand Elements: Start by defining key brand elements that represent your business and resonate with your target audience. This includes your logo, color palette, typography, visual style, tone of voice, and brand messaging. Ensure consistency across

all brand elements to create a cohesive and memorable brand identity.

2. Reflect Your Values and Personality: Your brand identity should reflect the values, beliefs, and personality of your business. Consider what you stand for, what sets you apart, and how you want to be perceived by customers. Infuse these attributes into your brand elements to create an authentic and compelling brand identity.

3. Choose a Memorable Logo: Your logo is often the first visual representation of your brand that customers encounter. Design a logo that is unique, memorable, and reflective of your brand's identity. Consider working with a professional designer to create a logo that captures the essence of your business and resonates with your target market.

4. Select a Distinct Color Palette: Colors play a significant role in shaping brand perception and evoking emotions. Choose a color palette that aligns with your brand values, personality, and target audience preferences. Use colors strategically across your branding materials to create a cohesive and visually appealing brand identity.

5. Develop Consistent Brand Messaging: Craft a clear and compelling brand messaging that communicates your USP, values, and offerings to customers. Develop a consistent tone of voice that reflects your brand personality and resonates with your target audience. Use this messaging across all marketing materials, website content, social media posts, and customer communications.

6. Create a Visual Style Guide: Establish a visual style guide that outlines the use of brand elements, colors, typography, imagery, and design principles. This guide ensures consistency in branding across

all platforms and materials, maintaining a unified brand identity that reinforces brand recognition and recall.

7. Engage Your Audience: Involve your audience in the brand-building process by seeking feedback, conducting surveys, and encouraging interaction. Listen to customer insights, preferences, and feedback to refine your brand identity and tailor it to resonate with your target market effectively.

8. Evolve and Adapt: Brand identity is not static but evolves over time to reflect changes in your business, industry trends, and customer preferences. Stay agile and open to adapting your brand identity as needed to stay relevant, fresh, and engaging in the eyes of customers.

By following these tips and guidelines, you can create a strong brand identity that effectively communicates your values, resonates with customers, and differentiates your hobby-based business in the marketplace. A compelling brand identity not only enhances brand recognition and customer loyalty but also lays the foundation for long-term success and growth in monetizing your hobbies.

In the next chapter, we will delve into the practical strategies and tactics for marketing your hobby-based business effectively to attract customers, drive sales, and maximize your income potential. Stay tuned for valuable insights, actionable tips, and real-world examples to help you elevate your brand presence and achieve success in turning your hobbies into a profitable venture.

Setting Up Your Income Stream

In Chapter 4, we explored the crucial aspects of branding, defining a unique selling proposition (USP), and creating a strong brand identity for your hobby-based business. Now, we will delve into the practical steps of setting up your income stream by establishing an online presence, leveraging different platforms for selling products or services related to your hobby, and implementing effective pricing strategies and payment methods. This chapter will guide readers through the process of launching their hobby-based business online, reaching a broader audience, and maximizing revenue potential through strategic pricing and payment solutions.

Setting Up an Online Presence for Your Hobby-Based Business

In today's digital age, having a strong online presence is essential for reaching a wider audience, expanding your market reach, and driving sales for your hobby-based business. Building an online presence allows you to showcase your products or services, connect with customers, and establish credibility and trust in the digital realm. Here are the key steps to guide you through setting up an online presence for your hobby-based income stream:

1. Create a Professional Website: Start by designing and launching a professional website for your hobby-based business. Your website serves as a central hub where customers can learn about your offerings, make purchases, and engage with your brand. Ensure that your website is visually appealing, user-friendly, mobile-responsive, and optimized for search engines to attract organic traffic.

2. Optimize for Search Engines: Implement search engine optimization (SEO) strategies to improve your website's visibility and ranking on search engine results pages. Conduct keyword research, optimize your content, meta tags, and images, and build quality backlinks to drive organic traffic to your website and increase online visibility.

3. Leverage Social Media Platforms: Establish a presence on popular social media platforms such as Facebook, Instagram, Twitter, LinkedIn, Pinterest, and YouTube to engage with your target audience, share content, and promote your hobby-based products or services. Create a content calendar, post regularly, interact with followers, and leverage social media advertising to boost visibility and reach.

4. Start Blogging: Launch a blog on your website to share valuable content, insights, tips, and stories related to your hobby niche. Blogging not only attracts organic traffic to your site but also positions you as an authority in your field, builds credibility, and fosters relationships with your audience. Publish high-quality, relevant, and engaging blog posts regularly to drive engagement and conversions.

5. Implement Email Marketing: Build an email list of subscribers who are interested in your hobby-based products or services. Create targeted email campaigns, newsletters, promotions, and updates to

nurture relationships with customers, drive repeat purchases, and generate sales. Personalize your emails, segment your audience, and track key metrics to optimize your email marketing efforts.

6. Offer Online Workshops or Courses: Monetize your expertise and passion by offering online workshops, courses, tutorials, or webinars related to your hobby. Create valuable and engaging content that educates, inspires, and empowers your audience to learn new skills, techniques, or knowledge in your niche. Use platforms like Teachable, Udemy, or Skillshare to host and sell your online courses.

7. Provide Virtual Consultations or Services: Offer virtual consultations, coaching, services, or personalized experiences to customers who seek individualized guidance, advice, or support in your hobby niche. Use video conferencing tools, scheduling software, and online payment gateways to facilitate virtual interactions and transactions with clients.

By following these steps and leveraging various online channels and tools, you can establish a strong online presence for your hobby-based business, attract a broader audience, and drive revenue growth through digital marketing and e-commerce initiatives.

Different Platforms for Selling Products or Services Related to Your Hobby

When it comes to selling products or services related to your hobby, there are several platforms and channels available to reach customers and generate income. Whether you sell physical goods, digital products, handmade crafts, or services, choosing the right platform can impact your reach, sales potential, and overall business success. Here are some popular platforms for selling products or services related to your hobby:

1. E-Commerce Websites: Launch an e-commerce website using platforms like Shopify, WooCommerce, BigCommerce, or Squarespace to sell your hobby-based products online. Customize your online store, showcase your products, manage inventory, process orders, and accept payments securely through integrated payment gateways.

2. Online Marketplaces: List your products on popular online marketplaces such as Amazon, eBay, Etsy, and Walmart Marketplace to reach a broader audience and leverage their existing customer base. Utilize the built-in features, seller tools, and marketing opportunities offered by online marketplaces to boost visibility and sales for your hobby-based products.

3. Social Media Shops: Utilize social media platforms like Facebook, Instagram, and Pinterest to set up shop and sell products directly to your followers and audience. Create shoppable posts, showcase products, and facilitate seamless transactions through social commerce features to drive sales and conversions. Leverage social media advertising, influencer partnerships, and engagement strategies to promote your products, engage with customers, and drive traffic to your social media shop.

4. Online Auction Sites: Consider selling unique or collectible items related to your hobby on online auction sites such as eBay, Heritage Auctions, and Catawiki. Auctions can generate excitement, competition, and interest among buyers, leading to higher prices and increased visibility for your hobby-based offerings.

5. Digital Marketplaces: If you create digital products such as e-books, digital downloads, templates, or software related to your hobby, consider selling them on digital marketplaces like Gumroad, Creative Market, Envato Market, or Etsy Digital. Reach a global audience, earn passive income, and monetize your digital creations through online platforms.

6. Subscription Services: Explore the subscription model by offering monthly boxes, memberships, or exclusive content related to your hobby. Platforms like Cratejoy, Patreon, Substack, and Memberful enable you to create subscription-based offerings, cultivate a loyal fan base, and generate recurring revenue from subscribers.

7. Local Marketplaces: If you prefer selling locally or connecting with customers in your community, consider platforms like Craigslist, Facebook Marketplace, Nextdoor, or local classified ads to promote and sell your hobby-based products or services. Engage with local customers, arrange pickups or deliveries, and build relationships within your community.

8. Online Communities and Forums: Engage with hobby enthusiasts, collectors, or niche communities by participating in online forums, groups, or marketplaces dedicated to your hobby. Share your expertise, network with like-minded individuals, and promote your offerings within targeted online communities to reach a highly engaged audience.

By exploring and leveraging different platforms for selling products or services related to your hobby, you can expand your reach, connect with customers across diverse channels, and maximize revenue opportunities through strategic multi-channel selling strategies.

Advice on Pricing Strategies and Payment Methods

Setting the right pricing strategies and offering convenient payment methods are critical aspects of monetizing your hobbies and maximizing income potential. Pricing your products or services competitively, profitably, and in alignment with customer expectations can impact sales, profitability, and overall business success. Likewise, providing secure, flexible, and user-friendly payment options can enhance customer experience, streamline transactions, and drive conversions. Here are some tips and advice on pricing strategies and payment methods for your hobby-based business:

Pricing Strategies:

1. Know Your Costs: Calculate your costs accurately, including materials, production, overhead, and labor, to determine a profitable pricing structure for your products or services. Factor in taxes, shipping, and other expenses to ensure that your pricing covers all costs and generates a reasonable profit margin.

2. Research the Market: Conduct market research to understand pricing trends, competitor prices, customer preferences, and demand for similar products or services in your niche. Analyze pricing strategies used by competitors and identify opportunities to differentiate your pricing based on unique value propositions, quality, or offerings.

3. Consider Value-Based Pricing: Price your products or services based on the perceived value they offer to customers rather than solely on costs or competition. Highlight the benefits, features, and outcomes that customers receive from your offerings to justify premium pricing and convey value to buyers.

4. Implement Tiered Pricing: Offer different pricing tiers, packages, or bundles to cater to diverse customer segments and preferences. Provide options for basic, standard, and premium versions of your products or services with varying features, pricing levels, and value propositions to appeal to a wider audience.

5. Use Psychological Pricing: Utilize pricing tactics such as charm pricing (e.g., $9.99 instead of $10), price anchoring, bundling, discounts, or limited-time offers to influence customer perception, trigger impulse purchases, and increase sales volume. Experiment with pricing strategies to gauge customer response and optimize pricing for maximum profitability.

Payment Methods:

1. Offer Multiple Payment Options: Provide customers with a variety of payment methods to accommodate their preferences and facilitate seamless transactions. Accept credit cards, debit cards, digital wallets (e.g., PayPal, Apple Pay), bank transfers, and alternative payment methods to cater to diverse customer needs and enhance convenience.

2. Ensure Secure Transactions: Prioritize security and data protection by implementing secure payment gateways, SSL encryption, and compliance with payment card industry (PCI) standards to safeguard customer information and prevent fraud. Display trust badges, security seals, and SSL certificates to instill confidence in customers and encourage secure transactions.

3. Streamline Checkout Process: Optimize your checkout process for simplicity, speed, and ease of use to reduce cart abandonment rates and improve conversion rates. Minimize steps, eliminate

distractions, offer guest checkout options, and provide clear instructions to guide customers through the payment process smoothly.

4. Communicate Transparent Pricing: Clearly communicate pricing, fees, taxes, and shipping costs upfront to avoid surprises and build trust with customers. Provide transparent pricing information on product pages, checkout pages, and order confirmation emails to ensure transparency and eliminate confusion regarding pricing and payment details.

5. Implement Subscription or Recurring Billing: If you offer subscription services, memberships, or recurring purchases, consider implementing automated billing systems to streamline recurring payments, manage subscriptions, and provide a hassle-free experience for customers. Use subscription management platforms like Recurly, Chargebee, or Stripe Billing to automate billing cycles and optimize subscription revenue.

6. Monitor Payment Performance: Track key metrics such as conversion rates, average order value, payment success rates, and chargeback ratios to evaluate the performance of your pricing strategies and payment methods. Analyze customer feedback, transaction data, and payment processing insights to identify opportunities for optimization and enhancement.

7. Provide Exceptional Customer Support: Offer responsive customer support, assistance, and guidance to address payment-related inquiries, resolve issues, and ensure a positive experience for customers. Communicate proactively, offer help with payment processing, and seek feedback to continuously improve your payment processes and customer service.

In conclusion, setting up your income stream for your hobby-based business involves creating a strong online presence, leveraging multiple platforms for selling products or services related to your hobby, and implementing effective pricing strategies and payment methods to drive revenue growth and maximize profitability. By following the guidelines, tips, and advice outlined in this chapter, you can establish a successful income stream from your hobbies, connect with customers, and monetize your passion effectively in the digital marketplace.

In the next chapter, we will explore strategies for marketing and promoting your hobby-based business, engaging with your target audience, and expanding your reach through digital marketing, content creation, and customer relationship management. Stay tuned for valuable insights, actionable tips, and practical techniques to elevate your marketing efforts and drive business growth in the competitive landscape of hobby-based entrepreneurship.

Marketing And Promotion

In the world of hobby-based businesses, marketing and promotion play a crucial role in driving brand awareness, attracting customers, and achieving business success. In this chapter, we will delve into the strategies and techniques that can help you effectively market your hobby-based business, utilize social media, content marketing, and networking to reach your target audience, and discuss the importance of building a loyal customer base for sustainable growth and long-term success.

Marketing Your Hobby-Based Business Effectively

Marketing is the art of telling your story, showcasing your products or services, and connecting with your target audience. For hobby-based businesses, marketing is not just about selling products; it's about sharing your passion, creativity, and expertise with the world. Here are some key strategies to help you market your hobby-based business effectively:

1. Define Your Target Audience: Understanding your target audience is the first step in developing a successful marketing strategy. Who are your ideal customers? What are their demographics, interests, and preferences? By defining your target audience, you can tailor your marketing efforts to resonate with the right people and attract potential customers who are most likely to engage with your brand.

2. Develop a Unique Selling Proposition (USP): Your unique selling proposition is what sets your hobby-based business apart from the competition. What makes your products or services unique? Whether it's your craftsmanship, design aesthetic, or personalized approach, your USP should clearly communicate the value you offer to customers and differentiate your brand in a crowded marketplace.

3. Create a Marketing Plan: A well-defined marketing plan outlines your goals, strategies, tactics, budget, and timelines for promoting your hobby-based business. Identify the marketing channels that align with your target audience, such as social media, email marketing, content marketing, and networking events. Set measurable objectives and key performance indicators (KPIs) to track the success of your marketing efforts.

4. Utilize Social Media Marketing: Social media platforms provide a powerful way to connect with your audience, showcase your products, and engage with customers in real-time. Choose the social media platforms where your target audience is most active and create a consistent presence across channels like Facebook, Instagram, Twitter, Pinterest, and LinkedIn. Share compelling content, interact with followers, and use analytics to measure the impact of your social media marketing efforts.

5. Implement Content Marketing: Content marketing involves creating and sharing valuable, relevant content to attract and engage your target audience. Develop a content strategy that aligns with your brand voice, showcases your expertise, and provides value to customers. Whether it's blog posts, videos, podcasts, or infographics, create content that educates, inspires, and entertains your audience while promoting your products or services.

6. Engage in Email Marketing: Email marketing is a cost-effective way to nurture relationships with customers, promote your products, and drive sales. Build an email list of subscribers who have opted in to receive communications from your brand. Segment your audience, personalize your emails, and send targeted campaigns that deliver value and encourage engagement. Use email marketing automation tools to streamline your efforts and track performance metrics.

7. Collaborate with Influencers: Partnering with influencers, bloggers, or industry experts can help amplify your reach and credibility within your niche. Identify influencers who align with your brand values and target audience, and collaborate on sponsored content, product reviews, or brand partnerships. Influencer marketing can help you reach a wider audience, build trust with customers, and drive brand awareness and sales.

By incorporating these marketing strategies into your business plan, you can effectively promote your hobby-based business, connect with your target audience, and drive brand awareness and customer engagement. Next, let's dive deeper into the importance of building a loyal customer base and how you can cultivate lasting relationships with your customers.

Building a Loyal Customer Base

A loyal customer base is the lifeblood of any successful business. Loyal customers not only make repeat purchases but also act as brand advocates, referring your products or services to others and contributing to your business's growth. Here are some strategies to help you build and nurture a loyal customer base for your hobby-based business:

1. Provide Exceptional Customer Service: Delivering exceptional customer service is essential for building trust, loyalty, and satisfaction among your customers. Respond promptly to inquiries, address concerns or issues with empathy and professionalism, and go above and beyond to exceed customer expectations. By providing a positive and memorable experience, you can create loyal customers who will return to your business time and time again.

2. Personalize the Customer Experience: Tailoring your interactions and communications to meet the individual needs and preferences of your customers can help create a personalized and memorable experience. Use customer data and insights to personalize recommendations, promotions, and communications. Show customers that you value their business and appreciate their loyalty by offering personalized experiences that make them feel special and valued.

3. Reward Loyalty: Implement a loyalty program or rewards system to incentivize repeat purchases, referrals, and loyalty. Offer discounts, exclusive offers, loyalty points, or special perks for loyal customers who continue to support your business. Recognize and reward their loyalty with personalized incentives that show appreciation for their ongoing commitment to your brand.

4. Solicit Feedback and Listen to Customers: Encourage feedback, reviews, and testimonials from customers to understand their needs, preferences, and satisfaction levels. Actively listen to customer feedback, address any issues or suggestions promptly, and use insights to improve your products, services, and customer experience. By engaging with customers and showing that their opinions matter, you can build trust, loyalty, and long-lasting relationships with your customer base.

5. Engage with Customers: Stay connected with your customers through regular communication, updates, and engagement. Use email marketing, social media, surveys, and newsletters to keep customers informed about new products, promotions, and events. Engage with customers through interactive content, contests, polls, and Q&A sessions to foster a sense of community and loyalty. By creating opportunities for two-way communication, you can build relationships and strengthen connections with your customers.

6. Build Trust and Transparency: Establishing trust and transparency with your customers is crucial for building lasting relationships and loyalty. Be honest, authentic, and reliable in your interactions, communications, and business practices. Clearly communicate your brand values, policies, and practices to build trust and confidence in your brand. By demonstrating integrity, transparency, and consistency, you can earn the trust of your customers and cultivate loyalty that leads to repeat business and referrals.

By implementing these strategies and focusing on building a loyal customer base, you can create a community of dedicated customers who support, advocate for, and contribute to the success of your hobby-based business. Invest in relationships, prioritize customer satisfaction, and cultivate loyalty to drive sustainable growth and long-term success in the competitive marketplace.

In conclusion, marketing and promoting your hobby-based business effectively, utilizing social media, content marketing, and networking, and building a loyal customer base are essential components of a successful business strategy. By understanding your target audience, creating compelling marketing campaigns, engaging with customers, and nurturing relationships, you can drive brand awareness, customer engagement, and business growth.

Remember that building a successful business takes time, effort, and dedication, but with the right strategies and mindset, you can achieve your goals and create a thriving hobby-based business that resonates with your audience and stands out in the market.

Thank you for reading Chapter 6 on Marketing and Promotion. I hope this chapter provides valuable insights and practical tips to help you market your hobby-based business effectively, engage with your audience, and build lasting relationships with your customers. Good luck on your journey to success in the world of hobby-based entrepreneurship!

Managing Finances And Scaling Up

In the world of hobby-based entrepreneurship, managing finances effectively and strategically scaling up your business are essential components of long-term success and sustainability. In this chapter, we will explore the importance of financial management for hobby-based businesses, offer guidance on managing finances related to your hobby-based income, discuss the significance of reinvesting profits for growth, and provide advice on scaling up your business through expanding your product or service offerings.

Managing Finances for Your Hobby-Based Business

Managing finances effectively is crucial for the success and growth of your hobby-based business. Whether you're a solopreneur or have a small team, understanding your income, expenses, and cash flow is essential for making informed decisions, planning for the future, and achieving financial stability. Here are some key strategies to help you manage finances for your hobby-based business:

1. Track Your Income and Expenses: Keep detailed records of your income and expenses to monitor your financial performance and track your business's profitability. Use accounting software, spreadsheets, or financial apps to record transactions, categorize expenses, and generate reports. By tracking your finances regularly, you can identify trends, analyze spending patterns, and make informed decisions to optimize your financial health.

2. Create a Budget: Develop a budget that outlines your projected income, expenses, and financial goals for your hobby-based business. Allocate funds for essential expenses such as materials, marketing, and overhead costs, and set aside a portion of your income for savings and investments. Monitor your budget regularly, adjust as needed, and prioritize spending that aligns with your business objectives and growth plans.

3. Manage Cash Flow: Cash flow management is critical for ensuring the financial health and stability of your hobby-based business. Monitor your cash flow regularly to track incoming and outgoing funds, identify potential cash shortages or surpluses, and plan for contingencies. Implement strategies to improve cash flow, such as invoicing promptly, negotiating payment terms with suppliers, and managing inventory levels to optimize working capital.

4. Set Financial Goals: Establish clear financial goals for your hobby-based business to drive growth, profitability, and sustainability. Whether your goals include increasing revenue, reducing expenses, or expanding your product line, having measurable targets can guide your financial decisions and motivate you to achieve success. Break down your goals into short-term and long-term objectives, track your progress, and celebrate milestones along the way.

5. Reinvest Profits: Reinvesting profits back into your hobby-based business is a key strategy for fueling growth, expanding operations, and reinventing your offerings. Instead of solely focusing on personal income or immediate expenses, consider allocating a portion of your profits towards strategic investments, marketing initiatives, product development, or business expansion. By

reinvesting profits wisely, you can position your business for long-term success and scalability.

Scaling Up Your Hobby-Based Business

Scaling up your hobby-based business involves expanding your operations, increasing your customer base, and growing your revenue to reach new heights of success. Whether you're looking to expand your product line, enter new markets, or diversify your offerings, scaling up requires careful planning, strategic decision-making, and a willingness to take calculated risks. Here are some strategies to help you scale up your hobby-based business effectively:

1. Diversify Your Product or Service Offerings: Explore opportunities to diversify your product or service offerings to attract new customers, expand your market reach, and differentiate your brand. Consider launching complementary products, introducing new services, or creating limited-edition collections to appeal to a broader audience and drive sales. Research market trends, customer preferences, and competitor offerings to identify gaps and opportunities for expansion.

2. Expand Your Distribution Channels: Broaden your distribution channels to reach a wider audience and increase your sales potential. Consider selling your products through online marketplaces, retail stores, pop-up shops, or craft fairs to expand your reach and visibility. Explore partnerships with wholesalers, distributors, or resellers to reach new markets and grow your customer base. By diversifying your distribution channels, you can maximize your sales opportunities and drive business growth.

3. Invest in Marketing and Promotion: Allocate resources towards marketing and promotion to increase brand awareness, attract new customers, and drive sales for your hobby-based business. Implement targeted marketing campaigns, social media strategies, and influencer partnerships to reach your target audience and generate buzz around your products or services. Use analytics and performance metrics to track the effectiveness of your marketing efforts and optimize your strategies for maximum impact.

4. Build Strategic Partnerships: Collaborate with strategic partners, influencers, or industry experts to leverage their networks, expertise, and resources to scale up your business. Seek partnerships that align with your brand values, target audience, and business objectives to create mutually beneficial opportunities for growth. Whether it's co-hosting events, cross-promoting products, or launching joint campaigns, strategic partnerships can help you expand your reach, enhance your credibility, and drive business growth.

5. Focus on Customer Experience: Prioritize customer experience to drive loyalty, repeat business, and word-of-mouth recommendations for your hobby-based business. Provide exceptional service, personalized interactions, and seamless transactions to create positive experiences that keep customers coming back. Listen to customer feedback, address concerns promptly, and go the extra mile to exceed expectations and build lasting relationships with your customers.

6. Leverage Technology and Automation: Embrace technology and automation tools to streamline operations, improve efficiency, and scale up your hobby-based business. Implement e-commerce platforms, inventory management systems, customer relationship management (CRM) software, and marketing automation tools to enhance productivity, optimize processes, and drive growth.

Leverage data analytics, artificial intelligence, and machine learning to gain insights, make informed decisions, and drive innovation in your business operations.

7. Seek Funding and Investment: Explore funding options such as loans, grants, crowdfunding, or angel investors to secure capital for scaling up your hobby-based business. Develop a business plan, financial projections, and growth strategy to present to potential investors or lenders and demonstrate the viability and potential of your business for expansion. Seek advice from financial advisors, mentors, or industry experts to help navigate the funding process and make informed decisions about financing your growth initiatives.

8. Monitor Performance and Adjust Strategies: Continuously monitor key performance indicators (KPIs), track progress towards your growth goals, and evaluate the effectiveness of your scaling strategies. Analyze sales data, customer feedback, and market trends to identify opportunities for improvement, adjust strategies as needed, and pivot direction to align with changing market dynamics. Stay agile, adaptable, and responsive to feedback to optimize your growth trajectory and drive sustainable success for your hobby-based business.

By implementing these strategies and focusing on managing finances effectively, reinvesting profits for growth, and scaling up your hobby-based business strategically, you can position yourself for long-term success, expansion, and sustainability in the competitive marketplace. Embrace challenges, seize opportunities, and stay committed to your vision to achieve your goals and take your hobby-based business to the next level of success.

Thank you for reading Chapter 7 on Managing Finances and Scaling Up. I hope this chapter provides valuable insights, practical guidance, and actionable strategies to help you navigate the financial aspects of your hobby-based business and scale up effectively. May you embark on a journey of growth, innovation, and success as you elevate your hobby-based business to new heights of achievement and impact in the marketplace.

Overcoming Challenges And Staying Motivated

Turning your hobby into a source of income can be a rewarding and fulfilling journey, but it also comes with its own set of challenges and obstacles. In this chapter, we will address common challenges faced by individuals who are looking to monetize their passions, offer solutions for overcoming these obstacles, and provide encouragement and success stories from hobbyists who have successfully turned their hobbies into income-generating ventures.

Common Challenges Faced When Turning Hobbies into Income

1. Time Management: One of the most common challenges faced by hobbyists looking to monetize their passions is finding the time to balance their hobby with other responsibilities such as work, family, and personal commitments. Turning a hobby into a business requires dedication, focus, and consistent effort, which can be challenging when juggling multiple priorities.

2. Financial Insecurity: Transitioning from a hobby to a business can bring financial uncertainty and instability, especially in the early stages of building a customer base and generating revenue. Managing cash flow, covering expenses, and investing in growth initiatives can be daunting for hobbyists who are new to the world of entrepreneurship.

3. Lack of Business Skills: Many hobbyists may lack the necessary business skills and knowledge required to successfully monetize their passions. From marketing and sales to financial management and operations, running a business involves a diverse set of skills that may be outside of a hobbyist's comfort zone or expertise.

4. Competition and Market Saturation: In today's competitive marketplace, standing out from the crowd and attracting customers to your hobby-based business can be a significant challenge. With numerous competitors vying for attention and market share, hobbyists may struggle to differentiate their offerings and capture the interest of their target audience.

5. Self-Doubt and Fear of Failure: Doubting one's abilities, questioning the viability of a hobby-based business, and fearing failure are common challenges that can hinder the progress and success of aspiring entrepreneurs. Overcoming self-doubt, building confidence, and embracing failure as a learning opportunity are essential for staying motivated and resilient in the face of challenges.

Solutions for Overcoming Obstacles and Staying Motivated

1. Set Clear Goals and Prioritize Tasks: Define your goals, establish priorities, and create a roadmap for turning your hobby into a successful business. Break down your goals into manageable tasks, set deadlines, and track your progress to stay on track and motivated towards achieving your objectives.

2. Develop a Growth Mindset: Cultivate a growth mindset that embraces challenges, learns from setbacks, and sees failures as opportunities for growth and improvement. Stay open to feedback, seek opportunities for learning and development, and adapt to

changes in the marketplace to evolve and succeed as an entrepreneur.

3. Seek Mentorship and Guidance: Find mentors, advisors, or peers who can provide guidance, support, and insights to help you navigate the challenges of monetizing your hobby. Learn from experienced entrepreneurs, seek advice from industry experts, and build a network of like-minded individuals who can offer encouragement, feedback, and perspective on your journey.

4. Invest in Continuous Learning: Expand your knowledge, skills, and expertise through continuous learning and professional development. Take courses, attend workshops, and read books on topics related to entrepreneurship, marketing, finance, and business management to enhance your capabilities and confidence as a hobby-based entrepreneur.

5. Build a Support System: Surround yourself with a supportive network of friends, family, and fellow entrepreneurs who believe in your vision, cheer you on, and provide emotional support during challenging times. Share your successes, seek advice, and celebrate milestones with those who encourage and uplift you on your entrepreneurial journey.

Encouragement and Success Stories from Hobbyists Turned Entrepreneurs

1. Emma's Story: Emma was a passionate knitter who turned her hobby into a successful online business selling handmade knitwear. Despite facing challenges such as competition from mass-produced products and limited marketing experience, Emma persevered by focusing on quality, customer service, and storytelling. Through social media engagement, collaborations with influencers, and

participation in craft fairs, Emma built a loyal customer base and grew her business into a thriving brand known for its unique, personalized knitwear.

2. Alex's Story: Alex was a talented photographer who struggled to monetize his hobby due to a lack of business skills and self-doubt. With support from a mentor and guidance from online resources, Alex learned about pricing strategies, marketing techniques, and customer acquisition tactics to launch his photography business. By showcasing his portfolio, offering photography workshops, and networking with local businesses, Alex built a successful photography business that catered to weddings, events, and corporate clients.

3. Sarah's Story: Sarah was a skilled painter who dreamt of turning her passion for art into a full-time career. Despite facing financial challenges and uncertainty, Sarah took a leap of faith by launching an online art shop and promoting her work on social media platforms. By engaging with her audience, hosting virtual art exhibitions, and collaborating with art galleries, Sarah attracted collectors, art enthusiasts, and commission clients who appreciated her unique style and creativity. Through perseverance, dedication, and a commitment to her artistic vision, Sarah transformed her hobby into a thriving art business that brought joy and inspiration to others.

4. Ryan's Story: Ryan was a music enthusiast who wanted to share his love for music by teaching guitar lessons and performing at local events. Despite facing challenges such as limited teaching experience and stage fright, Ryan embraced opportunities to improve his skills, connect with students, and showcase his musical talents. By offering online lessons, participating in music festivals, and collaborating with fellow musicians, Ryan built a successful

music education business and a loyal following of students and fans who were inspired by his passion and dedication.

These success stories highlight the resilience, creativity, and determination of hobbyists who overcame challenges, pursued their dreams, and achieved success in turning their hobbies into income-generating ventures. By learning from their experiences, seeking support, and staying motivated, you too can overcome obstacles, navigate the ups and downs of entrepreneurship, and realize your vision of building a successful business around your passion.

As you continue on your journey of monetizing your hobby, remember that challenges are inevitable, but they can be overcome with perseverance, resourcefulness, and a positive mindset. Stay focused on your goals, seek guidance when needed, and believe in your ability to turn your passion into a profitable and fulfilling venture. Embrace the journey, celebrate your achievements, and stay motivated by the joy and satisfaction that comes from pursuing your passion and sharing it with the world.

In the face of challenges, setbacks, and doubts, remember that every successful entrepreneur was once a hobbyist with a dream. By staying committed, adaptable, and resilient, you can overcome obstacles, achieve your goals, and create a thriving business that reflects your passion, talent, and unique contributions to the world. Stay inspired, stay motivated, and stay true to yourself as you navigate the exciting and rewarding path of turning your hobby into a successful business.

Thank you for joining us on this journey of growth, transformation, and success as you navigate the challenges and opportunities of monetizing your hobby. May you find courage, inspiration, and resilience in the stories, advice, and encouragement shared in this chapter, and may you continue to pursue your passion with confidence, determination, and unwavering belief in your ability to succeed.

Legal And Ethical Considerations

Running a business based on your hobbies can be a fulfilling and exciting endeavor, but it is crucial to understand and comply with the legal requirements that govern entrepreneurship. In this chapter, we will discuss the legal considerations for running a business based on hobbies, offer guidance on intellectual property rights, taxes, and other legal obligations, and emphasize the importance of ethical business practices to build trust, credibility, and sustainability in your venture.

Legal Requirements for Running a Business Based on Hobbies

1. Business Structure: When starting a business based on your hobbies, you will need to choose a suitable business structure that aligns with your goals, risk tolerance, and legal obligations. Common business structures include sole proprietorship, partnership, limited liability company (LLC), and corporation, each with different implications for liability, taxation, and regulatory compliance.

2. Business Registration: Depending on your location and the nature of your hobby-based business, you may be required to register your business with the appropriate government authorities, such as the Secretary of State's office or local business licensing department. Registering your business ensures legal recognition, compliance

with regulations, and access to certain benefits and protections as a business owner.

3. Permits and Licenses: Certain hobbies and business activities may require specific permits, licenses, or certifications to operate legally and safely. Check with local, state, and federal regulations to determine the permits and licenses needed for your hobby-based business, such as zoning permits, health department licenses, or professional certifications.

4. Tax Obligations: As a business owner, you are responsible for fulfilling various tax obligations, including income taxes, sales taxes, payroll taxes, and self-employment taxes. Keep accurate records of your income, expenses, and transactions, consult with a tax professional or accountant to understand your tax liabilities, and comply with tax laws and filing deadlines to avoid penalties and legal issues.

5. Employment Laws: If you hire employees or independent contractors to support your hobby-based business, you must adhere to employment laws and regulations that govern wages, benefits, working conditions, and workplace safety. Familiarize yourself with labor laws, employee rights, and fair employment practices to create a compliant and ethical work environment for your team.

Guidance on Intellectual Property Rights, Taxes, and Other Legal Considerations

1. Intellectual Property Rights: Protecting your intellectual property, such as trademarks, copyrights, and patents, is essential for safeguarding your creative work, brand identity, and business assets. Register your trademarks and copyrights to establish ownership

rights, prevent infringement, and enforce legal protection against unauthorized use or reproduction of your intellectual property.

2. Contracts and Agreements: When conducting business transactions, collaborations, or partnerships related to your hobby-based business, it is important to have clear and comprehensive contracts and agreements in place to define rights, responsibilities, and expectations. Consult with a legal professional to draft contracts for clients, suppliers, vendors, and collaborators to mitigate risks, resolve disputes, and uphold legal obligations.

3. Data Privacy and Security: In an increasingly digital world, protecting sensitive information, customer data, and online transactions is critical for maintaining trust and complying with data privacy laws. Implement data security measures, secure payment processing systems, and privacy policies to safeguard customer information, prevent data breaches, and uphold ethical standards in handling personal data.

4. Product Liability and Insurance: If your hobby-based business involves selling products or services to customers, consider the potential risks of product liability, accidents, or injuries that may occur. Obtain liability insurance, product liability coverage, and business insurance policies to protect against unforeseen events, lawsuits, and financial liabilities that could impact your business operations and reputation.

5. Compliance with Industry Regulations: Depending on the nature of your hobby-based business, you may be subject to industry-specific regulations, standards, or certifications that govern your activities and operations. Stay informed about industry regulations, quality standards, and compliance requirements to ensure that your

business meets legal obligations, maintains integrity, and operates ethically within your industry.

Importance of Ethical Business Practices

1. Trust and Reputation: Ethical business practices are essential for building trust, credibility, and a positive reputation in the marketplace. By conducting business with integrity, honesty, and transparency, you demonstrate respect for customers, employees, and stakeholders, and earn their trust and loyalty over time.

2. Customer Satisfaction: Ethical business practices prioritize customer satisfaction, fairness, and ethical treatment in all interactions and transactions. By delivering quality products, excellent service, and ethical conduct, you enhance customer experience, foster loyalty, and build long-term relationships with your audience.

3. Legal Compliance: Ethical business practices align with legal requirements, regulations, and industry standards that govern business operations. By upholding ethical standards, respecting laws, and complying with regulations, you reduce legal risks, avoid penalties, and maintain a lawful and ethical business environment.

4. Employee Engagement: Ethical business practices promote a positive work culture, employee morale, and engagement by fostering a sense of trust, respect, and fairness among team members. By upholding ethical standards in hiring, training, compensation, and workplace policies, you create a supportive and inclusive work environment that values diversity, equality, and ethical behavior.

5. Social Responsibility: Ethical business practices extend beyond legal compliance to social responsibility, environmental sustainability, and community engagement. By embracing corporate social responsibility initiatives, giving back to the community, and promoting ethical sourcing and sustainable practices, you contribute to a better world and demonstrate your commitment to making a positive impact beyond profits.

In conclusion, legal and ethical considerations are essential components of running a business based on hobbies. By understanding and complying with legal requirements, protecting intellectual property rights, adhering to tax obligations, and upholding ethical business practices, you can build a successful, sustainable, and socially responsible venture that reflects your values, integrity, and commitment to excellence.

As you navigate the legal and ethical landscape of entrepreneurship, seek guidance from legal professionals, tax advisors, and industry experts to ensure compliance with regulations, mitigate risks, and uphold ethical standards in all aspects of your hobby-based business. By prioritizing legal compliance, protecting intellectual property, and practicing ethical business conduct, you can establish a strong foundation for growth, trust, and success in your entrepreneurial journey.

Remember that ethical business practices are not just a legal requirement but a reflection of your values, character, and commitment to doing business with integrity, fairness, and respect for others. By embracing ethical principles, fostering a culture of transparency, and upholding the highest standards of conduct in your hobby-based business, you can inspire trust, loyalty, and admiration from customers, employees, and stakeholders who appreciate your dedication to ethical excellence.

Thank you for exploring the legal and ethical considerations of running a business based on hobbies. May you apply the insights, guidance, and best practices shared in this chapter to build a business that not only thrives financially but also upholds ethical values, legal compliance, and social responsibility in all aspects of your entrepreneurial journey. Stay true to your principles, lead with integrity, and make a positive impact through your ethical and law-abiding business practices.

Conclusion

As we come to the conclusion of this comprehensive guide on monetizing your hobbies, you have embarked on a transformative journey towards turning your passions into profitable ventures. Throughout this book, we have delved into the various stages of identifying, planning, branding, setting up, marketing, managing finances, overcoming challenges, and ensuring legal and ethical considerations in the process of creating a sustainable income stream from your hobbies. Let's recap the key points discussed and motivate you to take the next steps towards realizing your entrepreneurial dreams.

Summarizing Key Points:

1. **Identifying Profitable Hobbies:** We began by exploring the wide array of hobbies that have the potential for monetization. By helping you discover and evaluate your own interests and skills, we laid the foundation for selecting hobbies with income-generating possibilities.

2. **Research and Planning:** The importance of conducting thorough market research and crafting a detailed business plan cannot be overstated. By setting realistic goals, defining strategies, and planning milestones, you have positioned yourself for success in your hobby-based business.

3. **Building Your Brand:** Establishing a strong brand identity and communicating your unique selling proposition are essential in differentiating your offerings and attracting your target audience. Your brand is the cornerstone of your business's reputation and value in the market.

4. **Setting Up Your Income Stream:** From creating an online presence to selecting the right platforms for selling your products or services, you have learned the critical steps in reaching a wider customer base. Pricing strategies and payment methods play a crucial role in maximizing your revenue potential.

5. **Marketing and Promotion:** Effective marketing strategies, including social media, content marketing, and networking, are key to raising awareness about your hobby-based business and driving sales. Building and nurturing a loyal customer base is indispensable for long-term sustainability.

6. **Managing Finances and Scaling Up:** Sound financial management practices, reinvestment of profits, and strategic scaling of your business are vital components of growth and expansion. By managing your finances effectively, you pave the way for future success and innovation.

7. **Overcoming Challenges and Staying Motivated:** Challenges are inherent in any entrepreneurial journey. By cultivating resilience, adaptability, and a positive mindset, you can navigate obstacles and stay motivated in pursuing your goals. Drawing inspiration from success stories can fuel your determination and passion.

8. **Legal and Ethical Considerations:** Compliance with legal requirements, protection of intellectual property rights, adherence to

tax regulations, and upholding ethical business practices are fundamental for the credibility and longevity of your hobby-based business. By maintaining integrity and transparency, you build trust with customers and stakeholders.

Encouragement to Take Action:

Now that you have gained insights and practical strategies from this book, it's time to take action and embark on the next chapter of your entrepreneurial journey. The path to monetizing your hobbies is within reach, and with dedication, creativity, and a willingness to learn and adapt, you can achieve success in turning your passions into profits. Embrace the entrepreneurial spirit within you and seize the opportunities that lie ahead.

Additional Resources for Further Learning and Support:

To further enhance your skills and knowledge in monetizing your hobbies, consider exploring the following resources:

1. Online courses and workshops on entrepreneurship, branding, marketing, and financial management.
2. Industry-specific forums, groups, and communities for networking and learning from experienced professionals.
3. Books, podcasts, and blogs focusing on small business development, e-commerce, and niche marketing.
4. Mentoring programs or business coaching services to receive personalized guidance and support in your entrepreneurial journey.
5. Tools and software for streamlining business operations, managing finances, and optimizing marketing campaigns.

By leveraging these resources and continuously seeking opportunities for growth and improvement, you can elevate your hobby-based business to new heights and achieve your financial goals while doing what you love.

In conclusion, I encourage you to take the knowledge and inspiration gained from this book and translate it into action. Start implementing the strategies, setting goals, and building your brand with confidence and enthusiasm. Your journey towards monetizing your hobbies is a reflection of your passion, creativity, and determination. Embrace the challenges, celebrate the victories, and continue to learn and grow as you transform your hobbies into a successful and fulfilling business venture. Best of luck on your entrepreneurial path!

Appendix: Templates And Resources

In this appendix, you will find a collection of templates and recommended resources to support you in your journey of monetizing your hobbies and turning them into profitable ventures. These tools are designed to assist you in creating effective business plans, defining your branding guidelines, and developing successful marketing strategies. Additionally, the list of recommended resources will further enrich your knowledge and provide valuable insights into entrepreneurship, marketing, and business development.

Templates:

1. **Business Plan Template:** This comprehensive template will guide you through the process of outlining your business goals, target market analysis, financial projections, and operational strategies. Use this template to create a detailed roadmap for your hobby-based business.

Business Template

Business Roadmap Template for Hobby-Based Business

1. Business Goals:
- Define your long-term and short-term goals for the business.
- Outline specific objectives to achieve these goals.

2. Target Market Analysis:
- Identify your target audience based on demographics, interests, and purchasing behavior.
- Conduct market research to understand your audience's needs and preferences.
- Analyze your competitors and determine your unique selling proposition.

3. Financial Projections:
- Create a detailed budget outlining startup costs, monthly expenses, and revenue projections.
- Estimate pricing strategy based on market analysis and cost structure.
- Develop a financial plan for managing cash flow and achieving profitability.

4. Operational Strategies:

- Define your product or service offerings and how they meet the needs of your target market.
- Establish a marketing plan to promote your business and attract customers.
- Outline your sales strategy, distribution channels, and customer service approach.
- Develop an operational plan including production, inventory management, and supplier relationships.

5. Implementation Timeline:
- Create a timeline outlining key milestones and deadlines for each aspect of your business roadmap.
- Set measurable objectives to track progress and make adjustments as needed.

6. Monitoring and Evaluation:
- Establish key performance indicators (KPIs) to measure the success of your business goals.
- Regularly review and analyze financial performance, market trends, and operational efficiency.
- Use data driven insights to make informed decisions and optimize your business strategy.

7. Continuous Improvement:
- Foster a culture of innovation and adaptability within your business.
- Solicit feedback from customers, employees, and stakeholders to identify areas for improvement.
- Continuously update your business roadmap based on feedback and market dynamics.

Use this template to create a detailed roadmap for your hobby-based business, and adapt it as needed to align with your specific goals and circumstances. Good luck with your business venture!

2. **Branding Guidelines Template:**

Establish a strong brand identity with this template, which includes sections on brand vision, mission, values, tone of voice, visual elements, and brand messaging. Consistent branding is essential for building recognition and trust with your audience.

Brand Identity Template for Hobby-Based Business

1. Brand Vision:
- Define your long-term vision for the brand and where you see it in the future.
- Describe the impact you aim to make on your audience and industry.

2. Brand Mission:
- Articulate the purpose of your brand and why it exists.
- Outline the specific goals and objectives you aim to achieve through your business.

3. Brand Values:
- Identify the core values that guide your business decisions and actions.
- Explain how these values shape the culture and practices of your brand.

4. Tone of Voice:
- Define the personality of your brand through a consistent tone of voice.
- - Describe the style of communication you will use to connect with your audience.

5. Visual Elements:
- Create a visual style guide that includes your logo, color palette, typography, and imagery.
- Ensure consistency in design elements across all brand assets and communications.

6. Brand Messaging:
- Develop key messages that communicate your brand's value proposition and unique selling points.
- Craft a compelling brand story that resonates with your target audience.
- Establish messaging guidelines for different communication channels and touchpoints.

7. Consistency and Implementation:
- Ensure that your brand identity is consistently applied across all channels and platforms.
- Train your team members to embody the brand values and communicate in the established tone of voice.
- Regularly review and update your brand identity to stay relevant and aligned with your business goals.

8. Brand Experience:
- Consider how your brand identity translates into the overall customer experience.
- Create memorable interactions that reflect your brand values and resonate with your audience.

By following this template and customizing it to fit your hobby-based business, you can create a strong brand identity that resonates with your audience and sets you apart from competitors. Remember, consistency is key in building recognition and trust with your customers. Good luck in establishing your brand identity

3. **Marketing Strategy Template:**

Develop an effective marketing strategy with this template, which covers aspects such as target audience segmentation, marketing channels, content calendar, budget allocation, and performance metrics. Use this template to plan and execute successful marketing campaigns for your hobby-based business.

Marketing Strategy Template for Hobby-Based Business

1. Target Audience Segmentation:
- Identify and segment your target audience based on demographics, interests, and behaviors.
- Develop buyer personas to better understand the needs and preferences of your audience segments.

2. Marketing Channels:
- Select the most appropriate marketing channels to reach your target audience effectively.
- Consider a mix of online and offline channels such as social media, email marketing, SEO, content marketing, and events.

3. Content Calendar:
- Create a content calendar outlining key themes, topics, and publishing schedule for your marketing campaigns.
- Plan content types such as blog posts, social media posts, videos, and email newsletters to engage your audience.

4. Budget Allocation:
- Allocate your marketing budget across different channels and campaigns based on their expected ROI.

- Consider factors such as advertising costs, content production expenses, and tools or platforms needed for execution.

5. Performance Metrics:
- Define key performance indicators (KPIs) to measure the success of your marketing campaigns.
- Track metrics such as website traffic, conversion rates, social media engagement, and ROI to evaluate performance.

6. Campaign Execution:
- Implement your marketing campaigns according to the content calendar and channel selection.
- Monitor campaign performance closely and make adjustments as needed to optimize results.

7. Analysis and Optimization:
- Analyze the performance data collected from your campaigns to identify strengths and areas for improvement.
- Use insights to optimize future campaigns, refine targeting strategies, and enhance overall marketing effectiveness.

8. Customer Feedback and Engagement:
- Encourage customer feedback through surveys, reviews, and social media interactions.
- Engage with your audience regularly to build relationships and loyalty through personalized communication.

Utilize this template to plan and execute successful marketing campaigns for your hobby-based business. By focusing on target audience segmentation, strategic channel selection, consistent content creation, budget allocation, and performance measurement, you can drive growth and engagement for your business. Good luck with your marketing efforts!

Recommended Resources:

1. **Books:**
   - "The Lean Startup" by Eric Ries
   - "Building a StoryBrand" by Donald Miller
   - "Jab, Jab, Jab, Right Hook" by Gary Vaynerchuk

2. **Online Courses:**
   - Coursera: "Digital Marketing Specialization"
   - Udemy: "Entrepreneurship 101"
   - Skillshare: "Brand Strategy: Building a Brand from Scratch"

3. **Websites and Blogs:**
   - Entrepreneur.com: A valuable resource for business news, trends, and insights.
   - HubSpot Blog: Offers a wealth of marketing, sales, and customer service resources.
   - Neil Patel's Blog: Provides in-depth guides on digital marketing strategies and tactics.

4. **Podcasts:**
   - "The Tim Ferriss Show": Features interviews with successful entrepreneurs and thought leaders.
   - "Smart Passive Income" by Pat Flynn: Focuses on passive income strategies and online business tips.
   - "How I Built This" by NPR: Shares stories of entrepreneurs and the journeys behind their successful businesses.

5. **Online Tools:**
   - Canva: A user-friendly graphic design tool for creating branding materials and marketing assets.

- Google Analytics: A powerful tool for tracking website traffic, user behavior, and marketing performance.

- Mailchimp: An email marketing platform to engage with your audience and promote your products or services.

By utilizing these templates and exploring the recommended resources, you will be equipped with the necessary tools and knowledge to build a successful business around your hobbies. Continuously learning, refining your strategies, and adapting to market trends will be key to your sustained growth and success as an entrepreneur. Good luck on your entrepreneurial journey!

Made in the USA
Columbia, SC
28 July 2024